ALL THE TIME IN
THE WORLD

REBECCA GETHIN

CinnamonPress

INDEPENDENT INNOVATIVE INTERNATIONAL

Published by Cinnamon Press
Meirion House
Glan yr afon
Tanygrisiau
Blaenau Ffestiniog
Gwynedd, LL41 3SU
www.cinnamonpress.com

The right of Rebecca Gethin to be identified as author of this work has been asserted by her in accordance with the Copyright, Designs and Patent Act, 1988. Copyright © 2017 Rebecca Gethin.
ISBN: 978-1-910836-60-6

British Library Cataloguing in Publication Data. A CIP record for this book can be obtained from the British Library.

Designed and typeset in Palatino by Cinnamon Press.
Cover design by Jan Fortune.
Printed in Poland.

Cinnamon Press is represented in the UK by Inpress Ltd and in Wales by the Welsh Books Council.

With thanks to the Hawthornden Trust for awarding me a Fellowship which gave me the seclusion and freedom to write this.

Contents

To my mother, Rachel

All the time in the world

The visit

1

The last time I was taken to see her
I sat astride her tummy and she laughed.

Why didn't someone tell me not to put pressure
on her, or was I too small to matter?
        But I was two. She was mine.
When I asked, she gave me the strawberries
in the bowl beside her bed. She said she had too many.

        Sixty years on
        I am still in that room.

2

and afterwards, she wrote,
R didn't seem to mind leaving me.

It wasn't I who was leaving of course.

The letter, like the others, starts
with the day's name as if days
were what mattered,
not the date or the month

because there was only
now

to her and those round her bedside
who watched her leave a little more
each visiting time.

Fetch

You said you believed
it was a beginning not an end
and so when I read that seers say
a creature leaps from our mouths as we die
I wondered what quickened in you
as you died.

Were you a foal that feeling free
galloped away from its mother
only to come back and find it was you
who had gone?

Or a wolf that loped
from a thicket to howl in the snows
for the rest of the pack before tunnelling
into the lines of a fairy story?

Or a hare that zig-zagged across field after field
to find a new form, safe among tussocks?

Gratitude

is sometimes unspeakable. Written
in a different pen after some thought:
it becomes speechless

I am not ungrateful
but just don't know what to say

It is the only thing of good
but her voice trails.

Her sister's letter

tells her a dear friend is also terminally ill.

My mother replied,
I don't think any of it has been fair, really.
Or perhaps it was. I suppose I shall never know.

The words on the lines of the paper
look firm now she knows.

After all this time, I hear the sounds
of her laboured breathing

in the last letter that would have arrived
the following day.

Grace note

I suppose I shall never know. But...
        she didn't say
        much more.

Her darning needle ticked against her thimble.

That was as far as it went:
But...

        like the sound of a pebble dropped
        down a deep well. A thought
        changing direction. A monitor
        slowing its script, coming back, slowing again.

'Want' was a word forbidden by my grandmother

but my mother writes

I can't help wanting things to be otherwise

Such a fat little mole of a word to signify lack.
It burrows out its winding passages
within you, throws up want hills.
It wants so much from you
because wanting always wants more
and yet more. Starting as a thought
it grows in your vitals.
The flip side of its meaning
is to wane and to waste
but what my mother really didn't want
was to be found wanting.

otherwise

is what patches the space
of all that might have been:
the unknown potentials,
the unknown consequences,
an unspooling of years following on
from days spent according to plans
before all this happened
in an altogether other world.

Sorry

She's short-tempered
She thinks it's her shortcoming
her shortfall
her short sight

but really, she's
short-changed
short-circuited
short-term
short-winded
short-lived
short of ... a miracle

I don't know what came over me

Agitation

Sometimes, just a touch unravels
the fabric of the knit. However carefully
she darns the holes, the old stitches sometimes
pull apart, morphing into
a new hole. It's harder at the heel,
where the foot rubs inside the shoe.

It makes her want to rip it apart,
to scream at them all,
and she has barely the breath in her to weep.

I felt so miserably stupid and tired after going out
and that agitated me

There's nothing to be done.

Nothing to be done.

Nothing, so

I won't do it again.

Like origami

With their perished creases
care is needed to unfold the letters.
Each one is stretched
in a paper hospital
and demonstrates how to crease, fold
and smooth the creations
with precision. I try
to read the prescriptions
they secrete under the flaps
without adding any flourishes
of my own. But in my hands
all her birds and flowers
turn into different figures
of her sorrow.

One colour

she never wore.
Her mother didn't hold with it –
she wouldn't be seen dead in it.

I see her in sober greens and browns,
blue perhaps or grey.
But never scarlet or crimson.
No bright lipstick, no cherry shoes
(neither pointed nor heeled),
no poppy red dress or pleated rose skirt.
Nothing to draw attention to herself
so when the time came
she could slip away unnoticed.

Later, my father handed me a box
of her hankies, folded in triangles,
with her initial (the same as my own)
embroidered and bordered in red.

Something my father once told me

Reading her letters is to grope about
in a cave system of the past,
red as the innards of a body,
where the moist gullet sparkles
in the light from the mouth.

My ears, attuned at once
to the smallest noise,
are alert for the sounds of her life.

I want to know how far in the tunnel goes,
how deep the water. In the dim light
I pick out an alcove cut into the stone
for a candle and spot a brocaded moth
camouflaged by the furred red
on the wings, like an inkling
of an unborn, the one she never mentioned.

Truth

Mr D, the consultant, closes the door
and lays out the evidence
for the doctor-sister, Annette:
its sickening blockage of the pleural cavity,
how it has infiltrated the airways
and is corroding the bronchi
as it spreads.

A tumult at large
inside her sister.

'How much,' he is asking,
'should she be told?
And by whom?
It's up to you'.

Her bed is a small boat

almost adrift
as she rests her one long oar
to glide through the shallows.
She hears distant bells
in the current's chime and ring
along the wooden hull.
Fish watch the boat's shadow
as if it were a cloud passing.
Reeds repeat themselves
like prayer across the water.

She shores herself up between
the small berths of their visits
but when her breathing shortens
she can still watch their faces –
with her back facing the direction ahead.
The tide has not yet drawn her away.

Her shoes are landlocked
and cannot anchor her.

A new start

If you and Ben could go to see any houses that might happen …
if you both think it suitable, buy it … that would be useful.

My father bought a laburnum tree
dangling its golden flames at sunset;
a dark beech hedge surrounding the lawn
like a graveyard. Rooks haunting
the trees at dusk.

At night, the house creaked.
My bedroom door shone white
from the light on the landing.

The pattern of leaves on my curtains
almost came alive.

When a spider ran over my bare foot
I screamed for her.

Bonefrail as she was,

she carried the weight for those who would mourn.
She lifted each one with the strength of her voice,

held them together while she was present,
trying to find ways to save everyone

from the heavy burden of fall-out. Just as
she carried my sister and me,

lying on her side at night, tilting
her spine backwards a little.

After giving birth to us, she held our small heads
on the stem of our necks with her hand

and carried us from room to room. Wrapped
in a shawl in the crook of her arm,

she carried us up and down stairs and lifted us
into the pram, the bath or the car,

before the scales started tipping.

What did she teach me of dying?

All of the organs and structure of her body,
even the bits that linked her together
synapses, diffusers, cells and valves,
all coursing with her courage
after the end of the War.

Facing death as though it's a fireball
there's no escaping.
Facing it as though it's a pit
she must fall into.
Facing it as though a ferocity
ate her alive and slowly.

No other way than forwards.

Always singing,

my mother sang love songs
and ballads, victory marches and rain airs,
her voice flowing like a river
to the sea where she began on shanties
and charms for good weather. Her throat
sometimes a little hoarse but she cleared it
and carried on with melodies
from island to island. She crooned
cradle-songs and lullabies for newborns,
blessings for marriages, intoned hymns
and psalms for Sundays, dirges for the dead,
sang carols for Christmas and nursery rhymes
for us and when we clapped, asking for more,
she carried on singing till her breath was gone.

Frugality

She likes to be of use, so in her hospital bed,
my mother is darning socks with fine wool.
With the needle she draws the yarn over
and under her warp thread without causing
a pucker, checking the tension to mesh a flat disc
across the hole. Smooth as an obol.
By the time each is done, she'll have touched
the yarn all along its length as it moved through her hand,
felt its spring and heft. But before she finishes
her supply (there's still two ounces left)
she asks her mother to bring in more wool
of the same colour so she can keep mending
socks enough to last.

Just like her—

She could read a book
do crosswords
or paint her nails
but she prefers to work.
So, on the subject of mending socks,
she writes *I've all the time in the world.*

Exits and entrances

She waits for the interval to end.
The lights have come back on,
the safety curtain has come down.
Other people get up from their seats
and move about. They have things to do.
And she wonders
what will happen next
on stage. It feels like an always.
That's because it isn't an interval.

A short life

In her photos my mother never grew older:
she's remained the same sort of age,
looking just as clear as she did when
her face first emerged in the dark-room.

Whenever I visited one of my aunts
she used to hug me and smile,
almost in tears, 'You look so like your mother'.
But she hasn't said that for more than a decade.

Nobody finishes dying
till the last one to love you
has gone.

So when I die that will be
the end of my mother.

Re-write

When she said *I've all the time in the world*
I knew the story had to change for this to be so
and only I could tell it differently.

So, at the hospital,
the consultant, Mr D, puts it
to her doctor-sister –
'It's a bit of a gamble
but it's worked on mice
so it's worth a try
in the circumstances.'

She gets out of bed, feels a bit groggy at first on her feet
but my father walks with her to the car.
Soon there's singing again in the house
as she's at home with us, newly alive and giving us baths
and teas and later another baby arrives as well.
No-one ever says they'll kill my dog.
And it's all fairly chaotic and lovely
because there's both a past and a future.
She likes watching catkins and flower buds
open in spring and we bring her frogspawn
and earthworms. She plays tennis with her friends
and mixed doubles with my father at the Club.
When we're all at school she goes back
to being a solicitor. Of course, she has to deal
with our father but he's not as bad with her
as without and she's foolishly loyal.
She sees our children grow up and they love her
and there are nieces and nephews and cousins.
When she grows old I look after her
and right now she's being forgetful and repeating
everything. She's just got lost on her way home
and I'm ringing up my sisters
and saying 'Do you know what she …?'
My story, not hers.

More tests

My Dearest Mummy,
I'm only sorry that I have to be away
for a further three weeks, she wrote.

> *I'm only sorry...*
> to be an inconvenience/ a slug-a-bed/ a worry.

Mr D said he'll wait to speak to her sister
'since there is a doctor in the family'.
But Annette isn't due till Sunday. Or is she?

You mustn't worry over this do. You must not worry.
I'm not worried at all. I am not worried.

She is wheezing, coughing.
Something sharp jabs under her ribs
for which she has to keep changing position.
She can't exert herself.
Her lungs feel so tired.

Snowdrops

My mother speaks the language of snowdrops,
her accent frail and reticent though the words
spear frozen soil and poke from leaf litter.

Her sentences survive all weathers: pounded
and battered by wind and rain, chilled by frost,
they bounce back, irrevocably white.

Their drops of hope arrive in the dark days,
when the cold gives them strength.
What there's no word for, is death.

Go-between

My dearest Mum,
I hope you've forgotten yesterday's little incident —
at least in theory.

She elaborates no further.

Her husband, Ben, has a temper while they have none.
He wants her to himself
at visiting time. He hates to lose.

Ben is trying to be better in the way
he says things. Please try to have patience with him.
He's promised to be good.

But I will always have to live with how
they face one another. I am half of him
and keep them bound them together.

I know what they thought about him,
'We told her so. He isn't the right sort.'

In for tests

The address at the top, Duke of York,
sounds like a pub.
I may not be here long,
she wrote. But

the window is large,
the room is sunlit all afternoon
and Matron is very sweet.
The bed is comfy with stacks of pillows,
her new nightie much too swish.

       She doesn't describe
       what's beyond the pane.

Nightie

I am stumped by the nightie
she said *looks almost too swish.*

Was it boudoir blue with a lacy bodice,
or ice pink with frou-frou ruffles
in the shoulders and hemline?
Surely not.
Or sheer white with a ruffle at the collar
trimmed in a thin spittle of red?

She didn't make this one herself.
It was a gift. For going away with.
My father chose it for her.
Nothing could be too swish for him.

It can't be too swish to allow yourself
hope, but perhaps hope was almost
too much.

Everyday

She sits up in bed, pillows at her back
darning socks or writing letters.
In the square of sky from the window
that faces her she sees rain falling slant,
clouds moving but, in the distance, it's lighter.

After dark she doesn't see rain falling slant
nor the parting of clouds. But she knows they are.

Shortly before

When she ran the water to give us a bath
and checked the temperature with her hand
before lifting us in
we thought we were having a bath.

But our mother lived in a tall tower
with twelve windows at the top from which she could see
all of her kingdom and each vantage point
gave her a deeper and longer view than the last.

So she knew when she ran the water to give us a bath
and checked the temperature with her hand
before lifting us in
we were not just having a bath
and that I would remember this all of my life
but she kept that to herself and didn't say.

Long before (1943)

'There is no blood at operations.'
(Assertion from Annette, her doctor-sister.)

Tell her from me it's eyewash! I never saw so much blood and sickness …
nurses have to arrange it so that the doctor never does see blood.

As a VAD nurse she washed stretchers, sheets, gowns, aprons,
pillowcases, drawstrings, mackintoshes
        soaked in blood after eighteen operations,
blood endlessly seeping from the weave
        of the fabrics,
her knuckles and fingers turning red
        with scrubbing, with the gush of blood into water
at every thump and squeeze
        of the twisted rope of sheets, gowns etc.

When hung up to dry,
Matron arrived to inspect
every article for the smallest stain.

I imagine dried blood
under my mother's nails.

Her father's gift

Matron won't allow food in rooms
and saying you're hungry brings on
a tongue-lashing. So,
like a secret lump of guilt,
the jam she can't open or eat
sits in the back of her smalls drawer,
which, when opened or shut,
rolls the tin with a clunk
against the wood as if trying
to expose her dreams
of fresh strawberries.

Not long after

My love and a kiss to the kiddywinks
        is how she signed off.

That was my sister and me.
She popped us snugly
into the *kiddywinks* word like a playpen.
We were like nestlings in a tiny cup of a nest
in a cleft, made out of twigs, feathers and fur
with a mud dome to keep out the cold.

We ourselves knew nothing of the outside world.
We were in a nest for kiddywinks.

Probably our father was too preoccupied
and never found time to add
the spider egg sacs to the twigs,
as a father wren should,
so the hatchling spiders would feed on the mites
that attack the baby wrens and then get eaten.

Perhaps the air temperature fell too low
        at a crucial point
for the tiny insects my infant sister needed
in order to thrive. She was so small.

Without her mother's warmth
        at that point
she couldn't live long

leaving me in a world without

Fingertips

Her finger prints will still be on the sheets of paper.
The pressure of the pen, the slant and curl
of the letters are all hers. The same fingers

that stroked my forehead, buttoned my sister's shoes
and tied her hair ribbon and washed
the endless bloodied sheets after operations

in the military hospital. I see the pen
in her hand. The words she wrote clutched
at the edge of her precipice and, as she lost grip,

she slid a little further, saying over and over
she believed it wasn't the end but the beginning
and I want to grab her back and ask

'the beginning of what and for whom?'

But her fingers have slipped
into mine and the ink has run out.

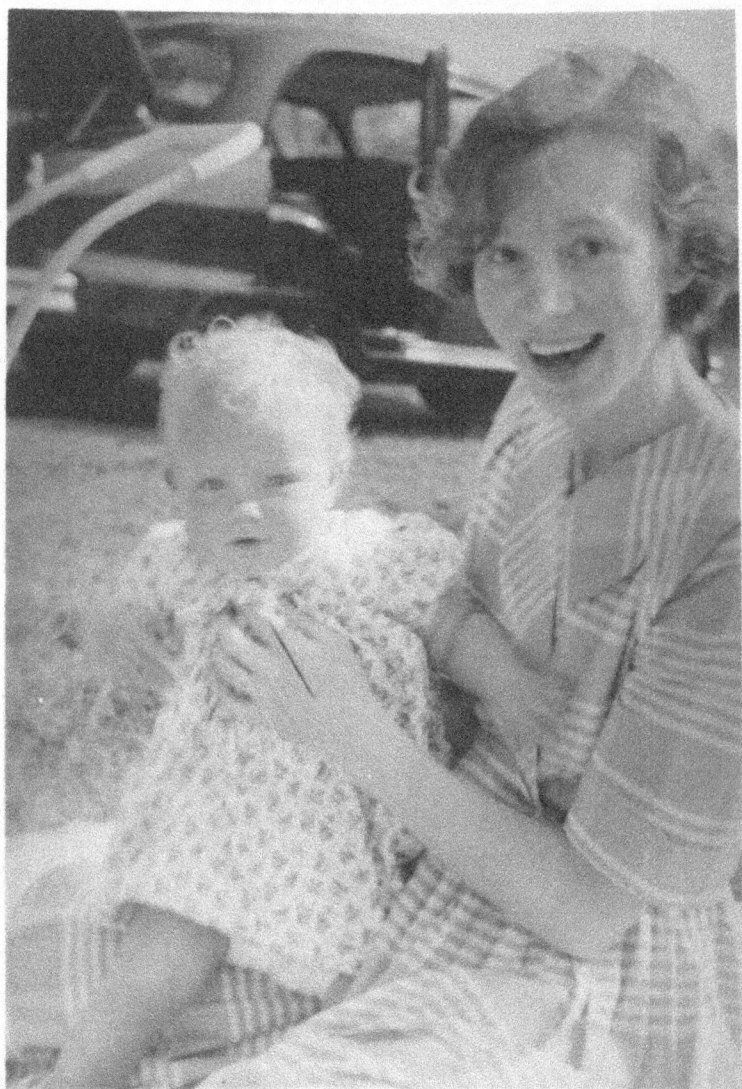

My mother and me, 1954